G000255286

True Love
Passion and Purity

by Fr Anthony Doe

All booklets are published thanks to the generous support of the members of the Catholic Truth Society

CATHOLIC TRUTH SOCIETY
PUBLISHERS TO THE HOLY SEE

Contents

Being Chosen in Love

Desire in the human heart

At one of the most poignant moments of His life Jesus made it very clear to His disciples that His relationship with each one of them had come into being through His personal choice and not theirs. 'You did not choose me, no, I chose you.' (*Jn* 15:16). Chosen to enter into friendship and intimacy with Him, they were to bear the fruit of mutual love that would be a sign of God's presence in the world. This public declaration of Jesus personally making a choice is extremely important as we begin to contemplate the mystery of love at the heart of human experience. The context of this declaration, the last Supper, where Jesus instituted the gift of the Eucharist, could not have been more significant.

The Eve of the Passover was a time of remembrance for the Jews when communal feelings, centred on God's salvific choice of His people, found a focus in the story of liberation from slavery in Egypt. The Covenant made with Abraham (*Gn* 12:2) and confirmed with Moses on Sinai (*Ex* 19) was central to the very identity that the Jews cherished as God's chosen people, and which Jesus made clear He was bringing to fulfilment in His own Passion and Death. The experience of choosing and being chosen, therefore, has been at the very centre of the Judeo-Christian understanding of the nature of religious worship. It is the living context in which the Covenant, the expression of mutual commitment has always found its meaning, as it brings alive the essential element of desire which alone can activate the interior world of the human heart.

Desire for love and for life

This makes perfect sense when we start to examine the way we develop as human beings, particularly in our relationships with others and in our natural search for fulfilment. In the very deepest sense our desire to be chosen by another in love, to be the sole object of their desire, is at the very core of our being. We have truly been created to respond to the other person's loving initiative and the whole structure of the human personality is built around this expectation. To put it slightly differently our human nature only comes fully alive when this deepest desire is activated, full of expectation and willing to respond in hope. The extensive clinical observations of mother/baby relationships have shown clearly how important it is for the baby to experience the loving attention of the mother from the earliest days in order to grow and mature into a loving human being. The manner in which the baby is held and the different ways that the mother responds to the baby's needs for attention and reassurance powerfully communicates the mother's love that the baby experiences as freely given. It is this spontaneous freedom of the mothers' response which is of vital importance for the baby's growth. Being free it affirms the essential goodness of the baby's core sense of being and activates the movement of life within the child.

The baby is the human symbol, for all of us, of powerlessness and dependence. If left alone for too long the yearning for love in the baby can gradually give way to a real physical and emotional fear of being abandoned. As the great child psychologist and psychotherapist Donald Winnicott pointed out, the unbearable anxiety of the child in this state eventually leads to a fear of being completely annihilated; such is the intensity of the need in the human being for the unconditional response of love that makes life and living literally possible. It demonstrates very clearly that the desire for love is synonymous with the desire for life itself and that real happiness cannot just be a passing experience but must be rooted in the development of the whole person. The mechanism for growth, therefore, that leads to ultimate fulfilment in love is triggered when love is freely given, when someone chooses to reach out and enfold another person through genuine commitment and devotion. It is then that an individual can become fully alive.

The intimacy of Jesus

Jesus in His choice of the disciple makes it clear that He is motivated by a profound love that has its origin in the Father's heart. Jesus is the 'beloved' of the Father because He is the 'chosen one in whom my soul delights' (*Is* 42:1), the one who has been endowed with Father's spirit 'that He might bring true justice to the nations'. It is this love that ultimately comes from the Creator that motivates His choice. 'As the Father has loved me, so I have loved you' (*Jn* 15:9). It is not just based on human affection, which obviously plays its part, but is rooted in the salvific love that the Father has for all His creatures. However, Jesus, through His own person, wants to makes it clear that from now on this love is not just to be acknowledged in some generalised way but to be experienced individually and personally. It is to have a unique impact on the person He calls into intimacy with Himself, calling them to a new level of love that will even give them the incentive to lay down their life for others. This will be possible because when Jesus chooses to love, His choice touches the very depths of the person's need to feel wanted and loved, evoking the mother and baby exchange.

This dimension is beautifully echoed again in the Prophet Isaiah when Zion says, 'Yahweh has abandoned me, the Lord has forgotten me.' Yahweh then replies, 'Does a mother forget her baby at the breast, or fail to cherish the son of her womb? Yet even if these forget, I will never forget you.' (*Is* 49: 14, 15) The experience of the Father's love, therefore, will be mediated through the personal choice made by His Son, to call into loving intimacy individuals who will experience this love entering into the very sinews of their humanity. It is in this experience of being chosen by Jesus that God will reveal His presence and the deepest yearnings of the heart will be fulfilled.

Self realisation: our need to be creative

When a person is chosen in love, growth and development begin to take place. Awareness of oneself, of others and a personal sense of identity begin to evolve. Desire for the experience of love is not just connected with the obviously pleasurable sensations of being the object of another's affection and the well-being that comes from the physical reassurance of love, but from the need that is central to our God-given nature which is to be creative. This exists deep within each person and reveals both a longing to express and communicate the mystery of one's being and experience to others, and the desire to give life and sustain it. In the immortal words of the Book of Genesis we are told that 'God created man in the image of Himself, in the image of God he created him, male and female He created them' (*Gn* 1:27). God has revealed Himself as Creator, but also has aligned the whole of humanity with His creative identity. When God chooses to call a person into an intimate loving relationship these needs, that are part of the God-like identity within us, are activated in a unique way. God's loving choice empowers us to full self-realisation and initiates a movement of life that wishes to express itself through communication and the generation of new life. Jesus has a unique part to play in this process.

Let us imagine, for a moment, God the Father as a huge diamond, Who every time a new person is conceived takes a fragment of Himself and places it deep within the person's heart. This fragment is a unique part of Himself, irreplaceable and unrepeatable. It means that deep within every human being God's image and likeness, His living presence, waits to reveal itself in order to communicate the very essence of His love in a way that gives life to others. This fragment is each person's buried treasure. The only person who knows where it is buried is Jesus Christ, God's only Son, and this accounts for the unique role that Jesus has in the life of every human being. In His priestly prayer at the Last Supper Jesus refers to the power that the Father has given Him over all mankind (*Jn* 17:2), the authority that was given its most profound expression in His self-giving on the Cross. It is Jesus alone Who has the power to bring alive this sacred image within us by first choosing us as disciples, and then, through a growing intimacy with us entering into the depths of our humanity with a love that is reminiscent of the tenderness with which a mother loves her child. How does He do it?

Allowing the love of God in

When someone chooses us in love, in order for us to respond and allow the love received to bring us alive we must be willing to surrender ourselves in trust. We have to let go of our defences and enter into that vulnerable state of longing which enables us to be receptive. This places us in a powerless condition which can be frightening, arousing the deepest anxieties within us. But this is not always so. Depending on previous experience, particularly our earliest days of mother/baby dependence, the powerlessness we feel can be full of exciting expectation, full of hope that the loving encounter ahead will bring joy and new life. It is here in this powerless condition that Jesus wishes to make His appearance in our life. It is in the vulnerable and most defenceless part of our being that Jesus can make His entry and begin the process of establishing His presence permanently within us.

Hence, wherever the Christian community gathers there is always somewhere the figure of Jesus on the Cross, the figure of God in His most vulnerable condition. The crucifix, with the dying Saviour nailed to the wood, is the Church's most sacred symbol. This is totally understandable since it is from the centre of Jesus' suffering and death that the call to intimacy and fidelity is made, echoed so powerfully in the words of Jesus Himself 'When I am lifted up from the earth I shall draw all men to myself' (*Jn* 12:32). To enter into the deepest recesses of a person's life, in order to bring them alive from within, Jesus cannot impose Himself on someone but can only make an entry through a mixture of attraction and invitation. Jesus waits to be invited, yet always having, in a subtle way, made the first move. He comes to reveal Himself but also with the intention of liberating the person and empowering them to live the life they have been given to the full. 'I have come that they may have life, and have it to the full' (*Jn* 10:10). Why is it, therefore, that all of us in different ways constantly have to deal with resistance within ourselves towards the One whose only intention is to bring us to this fullness of life through satisfying in the deepest possible way the desire to be chosen in love?

Origins of our fear and resistance

The answer is to be found in the fear, mentioned above, that exists side by side with the capacity to be loved and to love. It is a fear that all human beings know to their cost can quickly gain immense power and destroy the process of loving and replace it with violence and hate. It can also operate in a less dramatic way by robbing love of its creative drive to search for relationships and express itself through giving life to others. In other words it brings to birth a caricature of love that gives the illusion of fulfilment but in fact does not liberate the heart but keeps it undernourished and prevents it from growing. This, in many ways, is its most deadly form and the one that most of us have to contend with. Where does it come from and how is it maintained? If we return to the earliest experience of the baby we will immediately see the capacity for fear is present right from the start.

As I have said above, the first environment of love, that of the mother's response, is itself not always going to meet the deepest needs of the child. The absence of the mother, be it through illness, work commitments, the care of other children, or perhaps an inability to respond caringly to the child through defects in her own childhood, are all potential sources of neglect. This in turn can arouse panic and rage and all kinds of violent reactions in the baby which will then lead to further unbearable feelings of guilt and anxiety. Being a vulnerable dependent person who waits with hope to be chosen and loved is not a simple business. It can be fraught with pain and uncertainty and will not always yield opportunities for growth and development. Through anger and frustration survival takes on a new meaning when it depends more and more on the child's ability to contain its fear and assuage its emotional pain. What then begins to emerge is a complicated internal system of resistance to the experience of love from another person. It is not that the fundamental capacity and desire for love and generative relationships is totally destroyed but in many people there exist serious levels of impairment that will have damaged the God-given innate capacity for a trusting response.

Why Love can be so Difficult

The enemy of our human nature - Satan

*T*his must now be put into the context of salvation history. In the Book of Genesis we see Satan clearly targeting the very centre of our first parent's ability to live in complete openness and trust with God and each other. It is fascinating, in an almost macabre kind of way, to watch how Satan slowly arouses this fear and mistrust of God's love that one knows is rooted in the experience of innocence and joyful dependence. Fear becomes the basis of rejection, and fear becomes the substitute for loving trust. To be vulnerable and powerless in the world is dangerous. Since God, our Creator, is not truly respectful of out vulnerability and innocence we are indeed at his mercy and open to His choice of us in love, not for reciprocal relationship, however, but so that He can exercise His power over us. It is, therefore, important to construct life and relationships around other sources of security that shield the human heart from potential rejection and exploitation. We have inherited in our spiritual genes the experiences of our first parents and at the very epicentre of our createdness, where we are poised for loving encounter with God and each other, we are now vulnerable to the same experience of spiritual exploitation and the birth of fear that we see in the Book of Genesis.

It is not only through the failures of those in our immediate environment that we are driven into ourselves to construct what so often turns out to be a false reality, we are at the mercy of the spiritual presence of evil and malice that Jesus Himself encountered in the desert and later in so many forms in His ministry. Satan, the Evil One, the Prince of this World, has been revealed in the words of St Ignatius in his Spiritual Exercises as the Enemy of our human nature. Through his envy and hatred of God he is constantly poised to manipulate and deceive the most noble human striving to bring alive the image of the creator in each of us. He does this by using the human propensity to turn inwards through fear, in the face of human fragility and powerlessness, literally turning us into victims of our spiritual heritage. With what results?

Our fear of death, of not being loved

The fear that I will not be loved, that I will be isolated, rejected, that I have no value in the eyes of others and will never be another's person's choice in love, can turn human vulnerability into a nightmare. For some it becomes a terrifying reality and can lead to all kinds of personal disintegration from mental illness to physical violence and despair. For others it becomes the source of endless addictive behaviour patterns rooted in dependence on drugs, alcohol or sexual experiences. The deep yearning for human fulfilment opens up an abyss at the very heart of a person's life that becomes a tormenting emptiness if it is not filled with substitutes. Possessions, power, new experiences, even food are invested with the task of somehow offering meaning to life. And as we have seen in our own day the pursuit of pleasure and immediate gratification of all instinctual drives have lead to a trivialisation of human existence and the continual need to re-invent images of ourselves that become more distorted and debase the grandeur of human nature. Even where dramatic symptoms of a fear driven existence are not present there is a whole range of disordered responses that every individual has to endure. They might just be socially unacceptable, irritating personal characteristics that continually disrupt the flow of life and 'seem' to be incurable. They are indicators, however, of a broken world that has incarnated its presence deep within the textures of life, and point to a distorted reality that has both spiritual and physical dimensions that defy human effort to control or eliminate. They in fact reveal the need for a source of healing that can remove the powerful effects that fear can produce, but at the same time is able to confront the mystery of evil which preys on defenceless humanity in the person of the Evil One.

It is clear from the Gospels that no one came to know Jesus authentically until they had experienced Him as a healer. Except for His mother, all the disciples had to undergo a personal transformation that enabled Jesus to enter into the wounded recesses of their hearts. The clearest example, of course, is Peter, who was dominated by an overpowering ego that blinded him to his fear and human fragility. His fear of rejection immediately overtook him when confronted by the servant girl in the High Priest's courtyard. So powerful was this fear that he was driven to deny this relationship with Jesus even while Jesus was physically present. Whether it was fear of rejection that went back to his earliest life experiences which made him vulnerable to the manipulative power of Satan or just the ever present human weakness that could not tolerate public humiliation,

Peter's denial threw him into a state of deep anguished suffering. Human poverty and weakness has never had such a dramatic representation. But as we know his powerlessness before his own fear and his inability to heal himself in the end was his salvation. It enabled Jesus to reveal His love for Peter in the very depths of his human weakness and so establish an intimacy with him that has become the foundation of the Church's experience of healing and forgiveness. It is in His healing that Jesus reveals His power and transforms the potential source of human fear. St Paul in his letter to the Philippians sums it up well when he says:

'But our citizenship is in heaven and it is from there that we are expecting a Saviour, the Lord Jesus Christ. He will transform the body of our humiliation so that it may be conformed to the body of his glory, by the power that also enables him to make all things subject to himself' (*Ph* 3:20, 21).

The force of God's election on us

We refer to the experience of Jesus as Saviour in terms of healing. However, in the light of the totality of our human nature, as created by the Father, this term does not describe the experience in all its depth and accuracy. If we return to the story of Peter's betrayal and forgiveness by Jesus and look more closely at the Gospel texts we can discern another element at work. It comes at the end of the story of the two disciples who are accompanied by Jesus on their journey to Emmaus. They reach their destination and celebrate the Eucharist with Him and, as St Luke tells us, on recognising Him immediately leave and return to Jerusalem to be confronted by the words of the disciples, 'Yes it is true. The Lord has risen and has appeared to Simon' (*Lk* 22:35). Peter had obviously shared his encounter with Jesus with the other disciples. There is no written testimony of what passed between them or of any words spoken. However, it was an encounter of such depth that not only was Peter healed and forgiven but was empowered to witness to the other disciples in such a way that they believed him and in fact based their belief in the Resurrection on his testimony. Jesus, as with the other disciples, had chosen Peter as a disciple, but it was not until Peter had been able to experience Jesus' presence in the very depths of his weakness that Jesus' choice of him in love could activate the sacred image of the Father within him. As we have seen the sacred image is a sharing in the Father's gift of revealing the mystery of oneself to others in love, at the same time communicating life in a way that brings freedom and light to those around us. Peter's fear had prevented him from doing this. Only when it was completely unmasked could Jesus then take hold of it, release Peter from its power through his forgiveness, and enable Peter to truly experience the choice of Jesus' love.

Gift of self-sacrificial love

The depth of loving intimacy that resulted between them is movingly captured at the end of John's Gospel in the exchange between Jesus and Peter on the shore of Lake Tiberius. There is a particular intensity in the feelings that were present in both of them when, for the third time, Jesus asked him 'Simon, son of John, do you love me?' John tells us, 'Peter was upset that He asked him the third time 'Do you love me? and said, 'Lord, you know everything. You know that I love' (*Jn* 21:17). The exchange, however, was not only an acknowledgement of the intimacy and trust that had been established but was also the opportunity for Jesus to then go on and extend the scope of this love that had taken possession of Peter's life. After each question, 'Simon, son of John, do you love me?' Jesus responded to Peter's assent with the commands, 'Feed my lambs, look after my sheep'. Just as Peter's experience of healing and forgiveness had empowered him to bring alive the faith of his disciples, the personal experience of intimacy with Jesus was to be the basis of a new ministry of salvific love for the Lord's family.

This encounter on the Lake of Tiberius is, therefore, a paradigm for all called to be followers of Jesus Christ. Eros is the name we give to that joy of being chosen in love, of having the need to feel cherished and special fulfilled by the love of one's beloved. When this is touched and engaged by the love of Jesus it becomes the source of a new energy of love that can move upwards and outwards to search for the fulfilment and happiness in the 'other', in a relationship where the joy of self revelation becomes a mutual celebration. In other words a relationship where Eros is transformed into Agape, the gift of self sacrificial love.

Eros and Agape

Pope Benedict XVI has reflected on the presence of Eros in a powerfully illuminating way in his encyclical *Deus Caritas Est*. He points out that there is an exclusivity in Eros that has a possessive overtone, but this is only right. Loving intimacy with another is always private, always exclusive. Indeed we are enjoined by the Gospel to recognise this dimension of Eros in our relationship with God the Father in prayer. 'But when you pray go to your private room, and when you have shut your door pray to your Father who is in that secret place and your father who sees all that is done in secret will reward you' (*Mt* 6:6). Eros is ecstatic and is fired by the anticipation of emotional and physical pleasure. The Body in erotic love craves recognition and the fulfilment of its instinctual drives. These are powerful forces and can overwhelm an individual's search for loving encounter with the 'other'. The drive to fulfil them can easily become an end in itself and hence Eros has often been seen as an inferior and unhealthy form of love. In response Pope Benedict says:

> 'Eros needs to be disciplined and purified if it is to provide not just fleeting pleasure, but a certain foretaste of the pinnacle of our existence of the beatitude for which our whole being yearns.'

Purification and discipline become possible when it is placed in the centre of our understanding of the sacred image which has been implanted within us, our buried treasure. The self-revelation of the Father in Creation is intimately linked to his desire for relationship with us, culminating in union with the Trinity. The Father has revealed Himself as the life-giver of the whole of Creation and so His desire for us to live in union with Him means that He wishes us too to be givers of life, finding the real meaning of our existence as we are able to be faithful to this joyful transmission of life. Jesus embodies all the different aspects of the Father's creative desire to heal, unite, and empower the other to give life. It is Jesus Who finds our buried treasure, our creative Father-like image, and unites it to the love of Eros with its passion and desire and eagerness for satisfaction, in His own person. Eros then has the opportunity of expanding and moving into a more specifically oblative expression where the need to experience personal gratification in love is transcended and the needs of another person become the object of love. This signals the presence of Agape where the desire for self-revelation and the creation of relationship discovers a new dimension of altruistic concern. This can then carry a person into a mode of self-giving that gives life and seeks the happiness of another person. What is important is to maintain a continuum between Eros and Agape, an interplay that creates a dialogue between the need to receive and the need to give. As Pope Benedict says:

'The element of Agape then enters into this love, for otherwise Eros is impoverished and even loses its own nature. On the other hand, man cannot live by oblative love alone. He cannot always give, he must also receive. Anyone who wishes to give love must also receive love as a gift.'

Jesus integrates physical
and spiritual aspects of love

When Jesus enters deeply into a person's vulnerable condition one of His priorities is to become that bridge between Eros and Agape. He comes with the gift of His own glorified humanity in order to gradually integrate the physical with the spiritual dimensions of love. With the grace of His presence the exclusive drive for personal satisfaction in relationships is opened up in an agapatial response to the other person. One does not exclude the other but enriches the process of self-gift and the grace of receptivity. It then literally becomes possible to say that we love others not just in a human physical sense but 'in Christ Jesus, Our Lord.' His agency and presence embraces the experience of love by enabling the person to savour the buried treasure, which is deeply embedded in the fibres of their being. The desire to be chosen in love is in an immediate sense very much part of the experience of Eros, being a desire for the exclusive response of the 'other'. However, it must be recognised that often in its more mature form this desire to be the object of another person's choice in love can be an expression of a deep and selfless generosity: when the other person is needy and unable to contribute in a concrete and recognisable way to one's well being, for example, through illness, disability, or personal tragedy, and their choice is in fact an expression of total dependence. In a true sense we can see Eros and Agape fusing into an expression of a real fullness of love. This can only be made possible through the living presence of Jesus.

The living crisis of love in our Age

As has already been pointed out, when the state of vulnerable expectancy is either seriously disillusioned or crushed completely there arises the reflex response in the person that seeks to mitigate the pain and ensure that the anguish of desolation, if not totally eliminated in the future, is at least seriously reduced by careful self-management. This is the way Eros becomes the vehicle for all kinds of compensatory attachments and subtle forms of aggression that arise from the anger and frustration of a person who, in a very painful sense, has been disappointed in love. This is why the Evil One can find a real foothold in a person's life and close them off from any possible movement for change. In the general cultural context in which we live it is easy to see how this evil can take hold almost without appearing to do so. How often do we casually repeat the words from the Letter of St James 'money is the root of all evil'? Even with the simplest stretch of the imagination we know that money, for most of us, is the legitimate means for constructing a well-insulated personal world that maintains a static experience of Eros that is basically defensive and in the end sterile.

Our culture plays on the need for human security and promotes an image of human fulfilment that is based on material prosperity and the gratification of instinctual needs. This is at the root of what one might call a living crisis of love that we have seen emerge in many highly developed countries where the maintenance of prosperity has been tethered to the most basic form of self interest. Eros has been successfully sealed off from Agape and the living presence of Jesus is for many at best an irrelevance, at worst a real threat to human freedom. And yet if Jesus is the one who can grasp the dynamic power of Eros, destroy the Evil One's attempt to highjack its potential gift and carry it into a whole new form of expression through the grace of Agape, where will He find the most creative opportunity to make His presence felt? In other words where is the privileged place in human experience that will give Jesus the opportunity of entering a person's life and enabling the human heart to realise is full potential?

Dynamic role of Jesus in our sexuality

We have seen how the wound of loneliness and a sense of personal failure can engender a specific kind of openness of heart. Human vulnerability and poverty of spirit can give Jesus the opportunity of revealing His compassion and enable Him to establish a lifeline that can become the vehicle of faith. However, it can only take Him so far into a person's life since there is a place where He is able to go only if the person is willing to surrender themselves in the most hidden and intimate way, giving Him that total freedom that leads to real union of heart and soul, and that place is a person's living experience of sexuality. It is in playing a dynamic part in a person's sexuality that Jesus is able to incarnate His presence most profoundly in such a way that the person's humanity is liberated at the deepest level. It is only then that the sacred image of the Father can begin to reveal its depth and mystery, with the unique synthesis of Eros and Agape energising the beauty of a person's capacity to love in a joyful and generative way. It is now time to examine this dynamic and yet complex aspect of human nature that can bring so much happiness and fulfilment and yet also be the source of deep pain and destruction in a person's life.

Masculine and feminine

When we start to reflect deeply on the nature of sexuality we immediately encounter the presence of complementarity. The masculine and the feminine, body and spirit, the drive to receive as well as to give, the desire to be chosen as well as to choose, all participate in an energising movement that is at the heart of what I would describe as the aliveness of sexuality. This finds its focus in the power and drive to give life that likewise reveals a complementarity in the joy that accompanies the physical and spiritual experience of the transmission of life. The physical intensity of sexual pleasure can only be equalled by the depth and intensity of the spiritual joy that comes when a person is truly generative, when the spirit of one gives life to the other. This complementarity is, of course, part of the ideal. Sexuality not only reveals the potential grandeur of human nature but also is the forum in which we see, so clearly, the wound of sin and disorder that can destroy a person. It is where fear can be incarnated in its most subtle form, where Eros is subjugated most effectively to the need for personal pleasure and the very meaning of human life is robbed of its spiritual centre. This is why sexuality is in need of the divine presence of Jesus who alone can integrate its many parts in a way that brings harmony and peace to the whole experience of love. He can only do this if he is allowed into its very centre, its drive to create a communion of love that has the power to give life.

Tragic fragmentation of our bodily reality

With the advent of sin and the transmission of the ongoing spiritual wound that we all carry, human sexuality stands in constant need of redemption. This is so because it is rooted in the very essence of personhood that was tragically fragmented through the sin of our first parents. In the Book of Genesis we are told that man became a living being when God breathed into his nostrils the breath of life. This statement is literally foundational for our understanding of our own nature. We live because God has chosen us to live, but not as a separate entity from Himself but with His own breath of life animating our spirit. Furthermore, for man's goodness to be complete God created woman as his helpmate, his companion. This elicits the joyful cry of bodily recognition of Eve that then underpins the two following statements:

'This is why man leaves his father and mother and joins himself to his wife and they become one body.'
'Now both of them were naked, the man and his wife, but they felt no shame' (*Gn* 2:24, 25).

Authentic personhood participates in the very life of God, yet at the same time is able to embrace bodily reality as an integral part of the life of the Spirit. This in turn releases the dynamic movement towards physical union with 'the other' that is based on the God given gift of sexual complementarity. This is possible since defencelessness, symbolised by the nakedness of Adam and Eve, posed no threat, aroused no fear of exploitation, which could damage the spiritual and bodily communion for which we have been created. Finally this must all be placed in the context of the first account of Creation where man, side by side with all the creatures God made, is commanded to 'Be fruitful, multiply, fill the earth and conquer it' (*Gn* 1:28).

Life-giving unity in each person

Pope John Paul II in his reflections on the Creation texts has alerted us to this dynamism and life-giving unity of the human person that existed in Creation prior to the Fall. Man was created with the potential to realise this unity and live it faithfully by being challenged to make a choice, thereby activating his freedom. God, we are told, planted a garden in the East and:

'caused to spring up from the soil every kind of tree, enticing to look at and good to eat, with the tree of life and the tree of the knowledge of good and evil in the middle of the garden.' (*Gn* 2:9)

The tree of life is the common ancient symbol of immortality; the tree of the knowledge of good and evil is definitely, in God's eyes, a source of death to the creature He has created in His own image and likeness. In other words it is a potential means of destroying the creative unity of personhood animated by His spirit. God, we are told, admonishes Adam not to eat of this tree and so experience death. However, it is also clear that Adam nonetheless does have a choice and certainly does activate it in due course, revealing the true meaning of God's concern.

The effects of sin on us

Reading through the description of Adam and Eve's seduction into sin by the serpent in the Garden reference has already been made to the way Satan introduces the element of doubt concerning the genuineness of God's love. God is not to be trusted, as He has not told them the whole truth. If they eat from the tree of the knowledge of good and evil they will, in fact, far from dying become like gods themselves, knowing good and evil. God is obviously afraid that they themselves might acquire unlimited power and He will then lose control over them. Intimacy and trust in God had enabled Adam and Eve to live in harmony with each other, with a total and unquestioned level of defencelessness between them that had aroused no conflict or anxiety. It had enabled that communion of being, which had originally been imparted to them by God's inspiration of life, to unite them totally not only with Himself but also with all that He had created. They were totally at one with the whole richness of nature that surrounded them. Once they had eaten of the fruit it is fear that immediately takes over. Adam's response to God's question 'Where are you?' is immediate, 'I was afraid because I was naked'. We are taken immediately into the very heart of the effects of sin, fear of God and fear of defencelessness in relationships.

This is symbolised in three different ways. The first is that Adam and Eve, the man and his wife, hid from God among the trees. The effect of sin does not just express itself passively but actively by consciously excluding God from life and experience. The second is that Adam and Eve sewed fig leaves to make themselves loincloths to cover the genital area that defined their masculine and feminine identity. Being naked now carried a threat because genital sexuality had acquired a power that could be destructive. It is important to understand, in the context of our reflection, how the two are intimately linked. Finally, the harmony that Adam enjoyed with the whole of Creation, with its access to the tree of immortality, was shattered and replaced by physical labour and uncertainty as to his spiritual future. Hence the condition of original sin was marked, from its inception, by a fragmented reality that we have all inherited in our flesh and spirit.

The inner struggle

We see this operating in the human tendency to fall into self-contradiction, in its most simple forms, in the continual struggle to align intention with will, and in the incapacity to maintain perseverance in the face of difficulty or opposition. As creatures we can be filled with self-doubt about our value, in spite of the love and acceptance of others, and this tendency finds its strongest echo in the drive to constantly build up our own ego, even at the expense of those we love. This all points to the truth that there is a missing cohesive inner strength that can co-ordinate human energies with the call to live in a unity of flesh and spirit. Without it the consequences can be truly dire. Earlier I highlighted the severe effects of the emotional deficit that often affects mother/baby relationships, resulting in all kinds of damage to the growing infant. Fears of rejection, abandonment, deep uncertainty concerning self-value, a general impairment in the levels of trust, all of these can create a real fragility in a person's ability to relate and bond with others. This, as we have seen, can open the door to feelings of intense aggression, rooted in anger, directed towards others and the self, which in turn can induce powerful feelings of guilt and shame. When we place this within the context of the inheritance of original sin it is understandable how complex many people's basic reaction can be to their human nature. The desire to be chosen in love and to be able to love in return never disappears yet it is the very desire or drive that has the potential of propelling a person into a vortex of uncertainty and deep suffering.

It is now easy to understand the inner world of conflict that all of us have to carry in some form. If we allow ourselves to experience one set of feelings it is usually at the expense of another. Very early on we learn how to repress or ignore feelings that will result in some form of unbearable inner tension or which might elicit disapproval or even rejection from others. This requires splitting off genuine parts of ourselves and placing them where they are, for the time being, out of harm's way. However, repressed feelings are an 'alive' part of our very existence and when buried they require continual effort to keep them from erupting again into conscious expression. Energy has to be constantly used to maintain the emotional paralysis and this can rob a person of real freedom and spontaneity. They must be continually controlling their feelings and always be vigilant that the volcano that they are sitting on does not decide to erupt at the wrong moment. This is often the only way many people survive without being torn apart. Defences must be carefully kept in place in case the cocktail of desires and fears suddenly become overwhelming and the person is unable to contain the emotional trauma. Where the repression and splitting off of feelings has been particularly severe this can lead to serious psychological illness and result in a personal breakdown. This means that we are all, in some way, vulnerable to the spiritual effects of original sin which are compounded in the varying degrees of wounding that have been part of our earliest experience of relationship.

It is not hard now to see how easily the Evil One can enter into our personal world, exploit our weakness and get us to damage ourselves, even without us realising we are doing it. He does this by aligning himself with the fears that exist in us, exploiting them with the view to getting us to strengthen our defences in a way that then insulates us from experiencing any movement and change in our life. It is Satan's task to see that we live with ongoing internal divisions, at the mercy of repression and self-contradiction, walking steadily on the road that leads to spiritual death and the tragic destruction of our buried treasure.

> 'Knowing what was in their minds he said to them, "every kingdom divided against itself is heading for ruin; and no town, no household divided against itself can last"' (*Mt* 12:25).

The nature of Jesus' love for us

It is now possible to understand in a much deeper and more comprehensive way the implications of Jesus' words to His disciples, 'I chose you'. Once we accept that our personhood in all its dimensions, but especially in its sexuality, is a gift that has been sorely damaged and left wide open to the merciless contempt of Satan we are in a position where we can truly understand the nature of Jesus' love for us. He alone fully appreciates the fundamental goodness that exists deep within us which has remained buried within our humanity in spite of the effects of original sin. In other words He knows that there is a capacity to be united with His Father, through Him, and to live according to the inspiration of the Holy Spirit. He knows that we seek fulfilment through the complementarity that enhances the different aspects of our personhood but especially in the desire for sexual union and the joys of physical and spiritual communion. Most important of all He knows that there is a hidden yet beautiful desire in all of us to be totally open and defenceless with the 'other' that can, in a mysterious way, bring to birth new life in so many different forms. He knows because He shares in our human nature in all its fullness, with the exception of sin.

The joy of the Incarnation and the reality of Christmas, even in our troubles world, still have the power to shine out in the darkness. We celebrate every year that God, in His Son Jesus, is at one with us in our struggle for human fulfilment. Moreover it is through His own experience of human suffering that Jesus is able to understand the complexity of our woundedness and the power of sin, in ways that we will not be able to comprehend this side of death. In His Passion He encountered both the reality of evil and experienced its effects with the wisdom and power of the Holy Spirit within Him. It is Jesus alone, therefore, Who is able to penetrate the unique way in which every person suffers the effects of sin in their humanity. This underpins His choice of a person in love, when He draws them into a new relationship of fidelity and trust. It is the offer of an intimacy in which a new mode of being gradually comes alive as the love that Jesus has for the person effects an integration of all the fragmented aspects of their life. It heals the tendency to split off and repress conflicting emotions and frees up the energy to love through opening the heart to new relationships. Jesus literally becomes a new source of aliveness and fulfils His words for the graced individual, 'I have come that you may have life and have it to the full'.

True Love
A Radical Inner Conversion

Conversion of the heart

This is the point in our reflection when the whole question of conversion and the discovery of a new rhythm of life come into focus. Conversion takes place in so many different ways. For some it is literally a Damascus Road experience, reminiscent of St Paul's encounter with the Lord. A moment of truth breaks through the ordinary routine of life and there is that combination of intellectual clarity and the welling up of a new desire for God that envelops the person. For others it is a slower process, and rather than a quick turning on of a light, it is analogous with the growing light of day that brings with it a new perception of reality as it moves out of darkness into a startling new clarity. There are two aspects of conversion that point to its authenticity. The first is the realisation of the centrality of Jesus and a new personal awareness of His presence and His desire for relationship with us. This spiritual definition, however, in most cases proceeds from what I would describe as a touch of grace within the person's being. This will have been the work of the Holy Spirit and will have been manifested in a deeper compassion for others who are suffering and a desire to give of oneself in some way in loving service. They are living signs that a change has taken place in the quality of love that has established itself in the person's inner landscape.

Often the qualitative change seems slight, and almost goes unnoticed, but precisely because, like the mustard seed it is so small and unobtrusive its power cannot be underestimated. It is in fact where the presence of Eros, that attachment self-gratifying love, is slowly being carried outwards, gradually developing the connection with Agape, the 'other' focused love, drawing a person into a new mode of self-giving. We can see this happening naturally in a new or already existing relationship where we are drawn beyond the defined limits of generosity that have been unconsciously held in place. We suddenly find ourselves walking an extra mile with someone and moving into unchartered territory. The landscape does literally often change dramatically and the securities and structures, so carefully maintained, that protected us from unexpected demands, no longer can be controlled and regulated as they were in the past. A new sense of powerlessness then appears and it is here in this unfamiliar and unnerving space, where disorientation and fear can arouse deep anxiety, that Jesus is able to reveal His presence. He begins to walk side by side with us as He did with the disciples walking to Emmaus, mysteriously entering into this deep state of uncertainty, and it is through this encounter that a new love for Him begins to grow deep within us. This is the essence of conversion.

Love of another

Fear is present in all human beings and, as we have seen, conceals itself through the possessive form of Eros. The hunger for possessions, wealth, power, repeated sensual distractions, for adulation and even the love of violence, which has it own power to fascinate and excite, all these can possess a person and appear to mitigate the fear that is deeply rooted in the heart. In the loving embrace with Jesus Christ all these false attachments will not only be exposed but jointly removed through the collaboration between the individual and Jesus, and a new pattern of life will gradually replace the old. It is this collaboration that reveals the meaning of conversion, which is at the heart of the call to be a disciple, and it is through the gift of the Holy Spirit that the will and desire is roused to respond to Jesus' invitation at the moment of greatest vulnerability. The place in which the collaboration takes place most profoundly is in the experience of relationship and particularly where the gift and mystery of sexuality is present. It is here that Jesus repeats the commandment He gave to His disciples at the last Supper,

'Love one another, as I have loved you'

And the real implications of the Christian life then become fully apparent.

Jesus' love for us: from disintegration to true love

How can we describe this love that Jesus has for us and that He wants us to exercise in our relationships with each other? It is a love that can gradually take away the fear of our vulnerable, defenceless condition, at the same time deconstructing the different forms of defensive attachments that keep the fears in place. It is a love that heals the wounds of the heart, the painful experiences of the past and the self-damage that we have all inflicted on ourselves deep with our spirit, through sin and the hurt we have inflicted on others. We must always remember that Jesus, during His own lifetime was primarily known as a healer and wonder-worker. His identity as Messiah, the Christ of God, was recognised by only a few at the time of His death. We too will begin to experience His love initially in its healing capacity, bringing a new sense of peace, of tranquillity to the troubled unresolved area of our lives. It is only the beginning, however, of the loving embrace that will slowly penetrate more and more deeply into our being.

This initial healing touch is an introduction to a love that actually has power to transform every aspect of our existence, but as we slowly discover, it can only do so as we ourselves learn how to respond to Jesus' constant invitation to surrender ourselves more completely to Him. It is a love that not only heals but also restores to full health, and it is here that its dynamic power reveals itself. The key concept is integration. We have seen how the sin of our first parents resulted in a fragmentation of the Reality of Creation as God had willed it. Male and female, body and sprit, the joy of sexuality and the power to give life, all these different facets of human experience existed in a harmony that was animated by the inspiration of God. The sin of Adam and Eve did not destroy any of these component parts of personhood but separated the vital links that enabled them to give a joyful and peaceful unity to

human existence. The inheritance of disintegration
has subsequently shaped the development of human
nature and has particularly damaged the most
beautiful and mysterious aspect of God's image deep
within the person, the power to experience the joy
of mutual self-gift in a way that generates new life in
all its forms.

The healing of our sexuality

Human sexuality is the epicentre, the point of
convergence, where the fragmented parts of
personhood manifest most profoundly the need for
healing and a release from painful disorientation.
Sexuality in its biological drive for satisfaction brings
together, in a uniquely powerful way, the twin
elements of desire that characterise the body and the
spirit. In the drive for genital pleasure the body
yearns to celebrate its existence as a sexual entity. In
the yearning to experience meaning and fulfilment
the spirit can only realise the fullness of its desire
through giving life and sustaining it. Right from the
very beginning of Creation it was in God's plan that
body and spirit interact creating a unity in which
God's very breath, His divine spirit, could participate
in the living experience of His creatures, and
through this continue to reveal His presence. When
the body and spirit remain split off from each other

God's spirit of life, what we call the Holy Spirit, is unable to bring to birth a unity within the person that alone can then unify all the other aspects of personhood. This then prevents God from realising His dream of animating His creation through living at its very centre, in the human heart.

It is here that Jesus reveals His true role as Saviour. He comes, in the words of the prophet Isaiah (59. 12) as 'Breach mender' and 'Restorer of ruined houses'. His task is to gradually enable body and spirit to find a new relationship that gives the Holy Spirit a living context into which He can breathe the new life of divine grace. The person who experiences Jesus incarnating His presence within them receives Him in a heart that is being expanded in love, as Eros is transformed into Agape. The process of collaboration then begins to take place and the grace of conversion becomes the basis of a new way life. It is above all a gift of loving intimacy in which two people begin to work together to integrate the disparate elements of a fragmented humanity. It is a new covenant of love that is inspired by the personal choice of the Lord Himself. Jesus' intention is that this love becomes a mutual expression of choice where both parties find their respective homes in each other, echoing Jesus' words 'Make your home in me, as I make mine in you'.

Driving out fear

Jesus comes to bring sight to the blind and light for those who live in darkness and the shadow of death. Intimacy with Him will necessitate a gradual confrontation with the truth of our wounded humanity and the ways in which disorder and sin have established themselves in the structures of our life. This experience of coming to face the truth and acquiring a deep spirit of repentance can initially arouse the deepest fears of a punishing God Who is waiting only to condemn and reject us as unworthy of His love. It is the replication of the reaction of Adam in the Garden, who hid himself from God 'because he was naked.' It is the most fundamental manifestation of the effects of original sin that cries out for healing and transformation.

Now Jesus told Nicodemus quite categorically that He had not come to condemn the world but to save it. This is why the focus of salvation must always be upon the relationship of living intimacy which Jesus is offering otherwise the confrontation with sin has no context that gives it curative meaning. It remains a cold legal process governed by fear that can quickly lead to neurotic perfectionism and a concept of spiritual growth which is achieved only through effort and willpower. When a response to sin is understood in terms of surrender to Jesus and His healing power this enables Him to share with us the gift of the Holy Spirit Who can truly effect the process of redemption. It is the Holy Spirit Who slowly brings a new order to the way we respond to our human instincts. He teaches us how and when to gives our wounded humanity to Jesus in a prayer of faith, and will breath into our human desires a new element of grace. This is the place where Eros begins to lose its self-centred obsession with personal gratification and begins to open up to the amazing possibilities of a love that is transcendent and searches to give itself for the good of another. A love that is of its essence sheer gift, a love that drives out fear.

Our sexuality and inner life

This is now the place to reflect about the way Jesus can enter the mystery of sexuality and bring to birth a life-giving integration that will, in the end, affect all the other aspects of a person's inner life. As we have seen, after the Fall the two main areas of fear in Adam and Eve related to their relationship with God and their genital concern with each other. These fears were a direct result of the separation that had takes place between all the component parts of the sexual reality that God had created. Adam and Eve now experienced for the first time a new sense of vulnerability not just towards each other and God but towards themselves as they experienced a new awareness of the sexual forces within their own flesh. The fragmentary effect of sin had removed what we would describe as internal boundaries that naturally hold the passions of the body and the desires of the spirit in a state of harmony. An internal anarchy now prevailed that when provoked produced a form of defence that expressed itself through a desire to control and possess. It is here that we discover the origin of lust. The absence of sexual integration that has the Spirit of God breathing through it means that the drive for immediate genital gratification will rapidly take centre stage and will brook no opposition and as a consequence will attempt to dictate the rhythm of any relationship that is becoming emotionally intimate. Sexual attraction and the desire for genital pleasure have been created by God and are integral to the process of physical union. The answer, therefore, to both sexual anarchy and the desire for genital gratification that has become out of control is not a rejection or condemnation of the sexual drive but the creation of a new response that will begin to re-connect all the parts of human sexuality and enable the Holy Spirit to animate the whole person.

Recovering true chastity of heart

When Jesus authentically manifests His loving presence He always calls the person to face this area of radical disorder and begin to consciously share this with Him in prayer. It is part of the whole mechanism of fear to promote, however subtly, the notion that Jesus only comes to console and affirm in a non-demanding way. His deepest wish is for us to face the truth of our disorder with Him, so that He can remove any fear or anxiety that accompanies self-honesty. At the same time it is always the Lord's will that in the moment of redemption we experience a new form of consolation and peace. This is where God the Father makes His intervention; He sends the Holy Spirit into the human heart and enables a person to hear the words spoken by Jesus. The first word is spoken in the silence of the heart which incorporates the human experience of the person in their relationships with others. In other words, it is through the movement of love from Eros to Agape, as the heart expands its capacity to give life that the Holy Spirit brings a new sensitivity to Jesus' presence within.

The second is through the Word of Scripture where Jesus speaks directly out of His public ministry and especially from the accounts Of His Passion and

Death. As a person is drawn into a meditation on the meaning of the Gospel the Holy Spirit enkindles a new desire to identify with the Lord in His message of redemption and new life. Finally the Holy Spirit opens a person's heart to the power and meaning of the Church's teaching, especially as it relates to the area of sexual morality. This is perhaps the place where the Holy Spirit most needs to be recognised in His dynamic power to effect change and open the heart to the profound transformation that Jesus wishes to bring about in a person's life. It is the place, perhaps, where a real renewal of an understanding of Catholic spirituality needs to take place, in our own day, and it centres on a rediscovery of the gift of Chastity.

Jesus' desire to heal the wound of our sexuality by helping us to experience a new level of sexual integration centres on His command that we love others in exactly the same way that we ourselves have been loved by Him. The call to discipleship is a call to live in loving union with Jesus moved by the Holy Spirit, which then creates relationships with others that have the power to give life and restore the integrity of the personhood of others. It is nothing more, nothing less. It is God's will that in the struggle to recognise our own broken condition, particularly in the sexual area, combined with a willingness to allow Jesus to bring a new integration to birth in the way we live out our relationships, a greater capacity to love others will grow in the depths of our hearts. This new love, that is grace filled and has the power to transform others, is at the heart of what we call Chastity. Chaste love is life-giving love that brings alive what is good in the other person. It not only has the drive and focus of Eros but also the altruism and generosity of Agape since it communicates the mystery and tenderness of Jesus Himself. Chastity is indeed a pearl of great price. It is, therefore, the love that the Lord asks us to search for, especially in our own time, as it can be the most effective vehicle by which the Truth of the Gospel can be proclaimed.

Many people's attempts to grow in their capacity to love and sustain relationships have been shattered in recent years. With the gradual acceptance of all forms of artificial contraception the fragmented nature of sexuality has become institutionalised in our culture. The split between the genital and the relational, the procreative and unitive aspects of sexuality, has been slowly destroying many people's ability to appreciate the gift and mystery of sexuality in a way that can allow God to deepen His presence within them. A fragmented sexuality means that the drive for exclusive sexual gratification and the need for control begin to dominate the whole concept of relationship. When it is no longer joined to the act of giving life, 'having sex' not only becomes an end in itself it can also acquire a pseudo spiritual dominance that can actually destroy the Life of the Holy Spirit within a person. It can actually become an instrument of spiritual death as it prevents the love of Eros moving into the love of Agape which alone promotes human growth and development. Loving commitment to another then runs the risk of losing its sustaining power and relationships are no longer opportunities to foster the joy of the Holy Spirit but in the end become sources of pain and disillusionment.

True meaning of our sexuality

It is only Jesus Who can bring that fullness of meaning to human sexuality that enables the experience of human love to reveal the divine imprint of God's presence in each person's humanity. He does this by breathing the presence of the Holy Spirit into the human heart that is able and willing to receive the very special gifts that only the Holy Spirit can bestow and embrace the truth deep within, the buried treasure of the Father's image. It is this divine imprint, brought to life, that can reveal the gift and mystery of sexuality. It is only the Holy Spirit Who can integrate the drive for genital gratification into the deeper process of building relationships that have as their primary goal the creation of a love that seeks to give life in all its forms. In other words it is only the Holy Spirit Who can slowly transform a self-centred contraceptive understanding of sexuality into a generative desire for a complete surrender in love that truly reflects the love that God has for us. He does this by teaching a person how to restructure the expressions of intimacy that allow the transcendent movement form Eros to Agape to take place. By slowly inculcating the gifts that St Paul cites in his letter to the Galatians (5:22-23) love, joy, peace, patience, kindness, goodness, truthfulness, gentleness and self-control, the experience of human loving truly has the potential to become the place where Jesus and the Father can make their home. Sexuality then finds its true meaning as the physical and spiritual dimensions of human relationships discover a new connection where covenanted love is the privileged locus for the deepest experience of integration.

It is Jesus Who slowly enables a person to acquire a receptive disposition to these gifts of the Holy Spirit and He does this in two ways. Through the sacraments of Penance and the Eucharist Jesus offers a person the opportunity for healing the wounds and effects of sin and a personal encounter with Himself that nourishes the desire for loving relationships that will take the heart to a new level of self-gift. It is here that Jesus can begin to remove the fears that are responsible for behaviour patterns that keep a person defensive and dependent on all forms of self-consolation that in the end are transitory and ineffective. At the same time He can strengthen a person's resolve to make changes in their life that initially appear impossible even to contemplate. It is here that spiritual conversion actually takes place. Through Jesus' dual actions of healing and nurturing a new desire is born in the heart to receive the gifts of the Spirit and express them in the new love for others that is growing within. It is this grace filled experience that liberates and discloses the fear of powerlessness that allows the mentality of sin to maintain its dominant hold on a person's life. Joy and fulfilment can then be found in an act of surrender to another person's initiative of love, where being chosen becomes the ultimate source of empowerment.

Freedom and growth in the resurrection

The experience of sexuality as it awakens vital areas of human need and expectation, therefore, plays an enormously important role in this journey towards freedom and a real spiritual encounter with God. It is essential, however, that the power of the Holy Spirit is given the opportunity to integrate its yearning for experience and fulfilment into the wider context of spiritual development. This grace of the Spirit is in effect the gift of Chastity, where the heart and mind of a person gradually lives in communion with Jesus and shares His capacity to love others in a salvific way. It takes time to receive this precious gift and calls forth in a person a willingness to walk on a new pilgrimage of faith. The contraceptive response to sexual love and desire has taken hold of our collective understanding of sexuality and this sadly is true both within the Church and in our society in general.

It is only the power of Jesus working slowly in individual hearts freeing them from blindness and fear, gradually bringing about a new birth of openness and trust that can help a person begin to walk this new road that leads to the deepest freedom and new love for others. Just as the people of God in the desert needed the manna that nourished not only their physical strength but also their spirits as they responded to God's call, so too the Church, in our own day, is being invited to embrace the Eucharist with deeper devotion and new insight. It is truly being revealed to us as the nourishment necessary on this new pilgrimage of faith in which the gift and mystery of sexuality can once again shine out in the life of the Church as it transforms not only marriage and family life but all relationships of love where Eros yearns to be united with Agape. It is only Jesus' presence in the Eucharist that can speak to the heart and mind of the person, giving them courage to let go of contraceptive attitudes and ways of loving, enabling them to move into a way of life that brings together the passion of love and the fundamental truth of human nature.

Only the Eucharistic Jesus can do this as He alone embodies those two essential elements of authentic love, on the one hand the Passion of the Father's desire to be united with all his creatures, empowering them to love others and himself with the same love, divine Eros, and on the other the purity of response which is rooted in a transfigured humanity that has plumbed the very depths of the human heart, consecrated Agape. To be united with the person of Jesus Christ in the end can only mean an embodiment of a love that redeems not just the individual but also gives life to the world, and this can only take place when the gift and mystery of sexuality breathes with the new life of the Holy Spirit.

It is the grace of the Resurrection that brings Passion and Purity together into an eternal synthesis of love which reveals the full meaning of Christian happiness. It is the gift that Jesus longs to bestow on those he has chosen in love, those chosen to be His disciples. When we are willing to surrender ourselves to Him in our greatest vulnerability, in the core of our sexual being we are allowing Him that access to our humanity that truly enables Him to become the light of the world. It is then with His help that we can begin to embrace the gift and mystery of our sexuality and offer our hearts as the place where the healing presence of God can dwell. In that most intimate gesture of love, made in faith, we will then render the supreme service of love to the world and reveal the face of our loving Father.

A Way of Life for Young Catholics

Written for young Catholics who want to live their faith more deeply but are not sure what steps to take, this booklet contains practical, down-to-earth advice on many aspects of daily life, whether spiritual ('Prayer', 'Confession') or moral ('Alcohol and drugs', 'Dating and chastity') or emotional ('Coping with worry or suffering') or vocational ('Discovering my vocation', 'Finding a good husband or wife'). It will be especially helpful for older confirmation candidates, students, and young adults hoping to learn more about their faith.

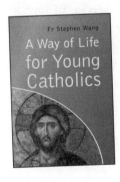

Fr Stephen Wang, a priest in the Diocese of Westminster, has worked in parish ministry, a university chaplaincy, and giving retreats for young people. He now teaches philosophy, theology, and pastoral studies at Allen Hall Seminary in London.

ISBN: 978 1 86082 487 6

CTS Code: Do 774

Don't be afraid to be Saints

Since beginning in 1984, WYD has drawn millions of young people to various locations around the globe, to 'meet Peter', and to think deeply about what it means to be a young Christian in today's world. With 'WYD Sydney 2008' in mind, pilgrims will find great encouragement here from the words of John Paul II and Benedict XVI, scrutinising the essence of what it means to be Christian today: Love, Service, Courage, Vocation, and making the right choices.

ISBN: 978 1 86082 488 3

CTS Code: Do 775

Informative Catholic Reading

We hope that you have enjoyed reading this booklet.

If you would like to find out more about CTS booklets - we'll send you our free information pack and catalogue.

Please send us your details:

Name ....

Address ....

....

....

Postcode ....

Telephone..

Email ....

Send to: CTS, 40-46 Harleyford Road,
            Vauxhall, London
            SE11 5AY

Tel: 020 7640 0042
Fax: 020 7640 0046
Email: info@cts-online.org.uk